Tiny Ti...

for You,
Son

Illustrations by Jeannie Mooney

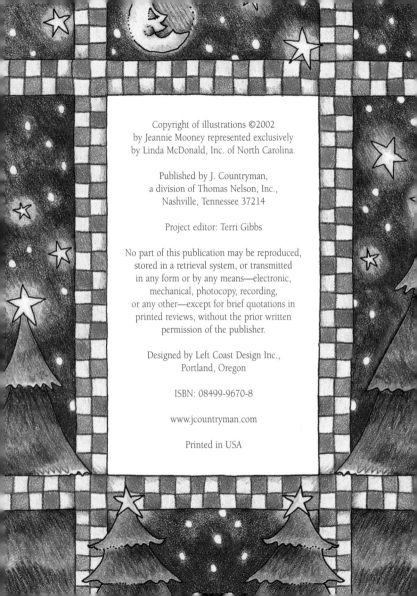

Published by J. Countryman,
a division of Thomas Nelson, Inc.,
Nashville, Tennessee 37214

Project editor: Terri Gibbs

Designed by Left Coast Design Inc.,
Portland, Oregon

ISBN: 08499-9670-8

www.jcountryman.com

Printed in USA

Tiny tidings
sent to say,
"I think
you're special
in every
way!"

From the moment Christmas starts, it pours joy into our hearts.

Here are some things
I find delightful about you:

_____

_____

_____

_____

_____

_____

_____

_____

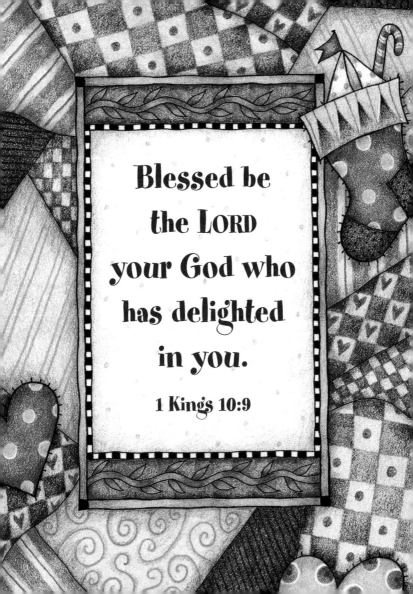

Blessed be the LORD your God who has delighted in you.

1 Kings 10:9

Love rained down
from heaven
on Christmas long ago.
God sent His Son
so we could know
that He loves us so.

May your heart
feel the joy
and welcome
the love that
God sent down
from heaven above.

Friendly laughter
across the miles,
A hug and
happy smiles,
It's a time of
joyful cheer...
Hooray!!!
Christmas is here!!

Peace at Christmas...and all the year through.

Though simple
and small
the greatest
gifts of all
are the ones
that come straight
from the heart.

Here are some gifts
from my heart to yours:

_____

_____

_____

_____

_____

_____

_____

_____

_____

©jeannie mooney

Holiday Greetings

Candy gumdrops

green and red,

Yummy smells

of gingerbread,

A chance to tell

folks near and far,

Just how great

I think you are!

Be merry

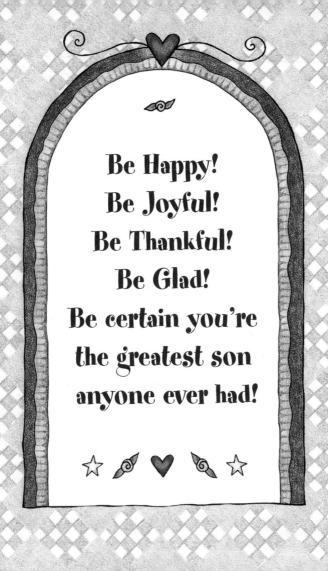

Be Happy!
Be Joyful!
Be Thankful!
Be Glad!
Be certain you're
the greatest son
anyone ever had!

©Jeannie Mooney

A son
is a gift
from
heaven.

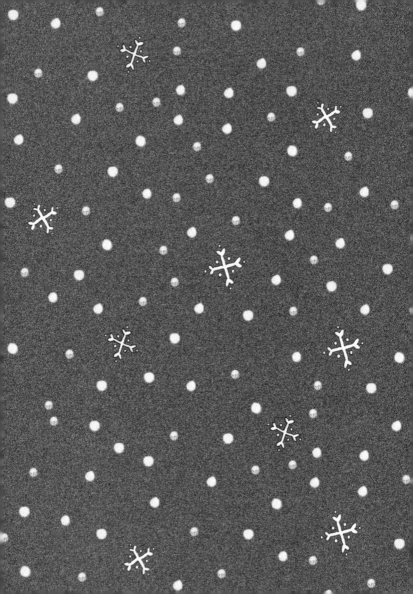